The Road Safety Officer

Diana Bentley
Reading Consultant
University of Reading

Photographs by
Tim Woodcock

My School

The Class Teacher
The Dinner Ladies
The Lollipop Man
The Road Safety Officer
The School Caretaker
The School Secretary

First published in 1987 by
Wayland (Publishers) Limited
61 Western Road, Hove
East Sussex, BN3 1JD, England

British Library Cataloguing in Publication Data
Bentley, Diana
   The road safety officer. – (My school).
   1. Schools – Juvenile literature
   I. Title   II. Series
   371   LA132
ISBN 1–85210–033–8

Phototypeset by
Kalligraphics Limited
Redhill, Surrey
Printed and bound by
Casterman S.A., Belgium

Contents

All the words that appear
in **bold** are explained in the
glossary on page 28.

Hello, my name is Mrs Hurst. I am a road safety officer.

My name is Mrs Hurst, and I am a road safety officer. After you are nine I can test you to see that you can cycle safely. Roads are dangerous places and riding a cycle on them needs careful practice. But it can also be fun. Today I am visiting a school in Reading.

I check Caroline's cycle before she rides it.

Before you ride your cycle you must make sure that it is safe to use. I check that Caroline's brakes work and that nothing is loose. I also check that Mark's tyres have a good **tread** and are pumped up and that the chain is not loose. Remember, you should never ride a cycle that is too big or too small for you.

I ask Dominic to start cycling without wobbling.

Dominic wheels his cycle to the **kerb**. He gets on it and waits. He looks all round for **traffic**. When it is safe to move he signals with his right arm and cycles away without wobbling.

Mark and Caroline cycle along the road correctly.

When cycling along you must keep both
feet on the **pedals**. Keep both hands on the
handlebars unless you are signalling.
Mark and Caroline cycle along the road
keeping near to the left-hand kerb.

Mark stops safely. First he looks behind him.

When cycling in traffic do not cycle so close to a **vehicle** that you cannot stop safely. Before he stops Mark first looks behind over his right shoulder. He then

signals that he wants to stop. He puts both hands on the handlebars and brakes. He steers the cycle to the kerb and gets off it.

Mark turns left into another road.

Mark wants to turn left. He first looks over his right shoulder and gives a left arm signal. He slows down at the **junction** looking for traffic. If the road is clear he turns left. He must not hit the kerb or swing out into the road.

Mark cycles into a right turn on a quiet road.

It is more difficult to turn right. Mark looks
behind him, signals clearly and cycles
towards the middle of the road. As there is
no traffic, he turns right at the junction
without stopping. He does not cut the
corner. If there is traffic you should stop at
the junction and restart when it is clear.
Remember to look behind you again.

Caroline turns right at a busy junction.

If it is a busy road it is often safer to stop on the left-hand side of the road. Caroline gets off her cycle at the kerb and waits for a gap in the traffic. When it is safe to cross she can walk her cycle across the road. Then she can get back on her cycle again.

Mark overtakes safely and gives the vehicle plenty of room.

Mark needs to **overtake** a stationary
vehicle. He makes sure the road is clear in
front and behind before he moves out. He
gives the vehicle plenty of room. After
passing he returns to the correct road
position. Never overtake when it is not
safe to do so or when you cannot see
ahead clearly.

Make sure that you learn the Highway Code.

You must learn and understand the road traffic signs and markings. I test you on the **Highway Code**. At the end of the test I tell you if you have passed. Remember

that passing the test is only the start. You
need to practise carefully on quiet roads
as often as possible.

Glossary

Handlebars The bar at the front of the cycle that you steer with.

Highway Code A set of rules for road users.

Junction A place where two roads meet.

Kerb The edge of the pavement.

Overtake To pass a cycle or car in the road.

Pedals You push with your feet on these to make the wheels go round.

Traffic All the cars, lorries and cycles using the road.

Tread The part of the tyre that touches the road. It should have a good firm grip on the road.

Vehicle A form of transport, such as a car or cycle.

Books to read

A Day with a Teacher by Chris Fairclough
(Wayland, 1982)

At School by Nita and Terry Burton
(Macdonald Educational, 1981)

Going to School by Alistair Ross (A. & C.
Black, 1982)

The Lollipop Man by Diana Bentley
(Wayland, 1987)

Safety on the Road by Dorothy Baldwin
and Claire Lister (Wayland, 1986)

The Teacher by Anne Stewart (Hamish
Hamilton, 1986)

Acknowledgements

The author and publishers would like to thank the headmaster, staff and pupils of St. Peter's Church of England School, Earley, Reading, Berkshire, and the County Road Safety Group, Department of Highways & Planning, Royal County of Berkshire.

29

Index

brakes 11, 17

chain 11
corner 21

handlebars 15, 17
Highway Code 26

junction 19, 21, 22

kerb 13, 15, 17, 19,
    22

overtake 24, 25

pedals 15

road safety officer 9

signal 13, 17, 19, 21

traffic 13, 16, 21, 22
tread 11
tyres 11

vehicle 16, 24, 25